I0759564

THINGS TO DO NOW THAT YOU'RE A GRANDPARENT

First published in Great Britain in 2009 by Spruce, an imprint of Octopus Publishing Group Ltd
Carmelite House
50 Victoria Embankment
London EC4Y 0DZ
www.octopusbooks.co.uk

An Hachette UK Company
www.hachette.co.uk

The authorized representative in the EEA is Hachette Ireland,
8 Castlecourt Centre,
Dublin 15,
D15 YF6A, Ireland
(email: info@hbgi.ie)

This edition published in 2025 by Hamlyn

Distributed in the US by
Hachette Book Group
1290 Avenue of the Americas
4th and 5th Floors
New York, NY 10104

Distributed in Canada by
Canadian Manda Group
664 Annette St.
Toronto, Ontario,
Canada M6S 2C8

ISBN 978-0-60063-964-0
eISBN 978-0-60063-978-7

A CIP catalogue record for this book is available from the British Library.

Printed and bound in China

10 9 8 7 6 5 4 3 2 1

Publisher: Lucy Pessell
Designer: Dani Leigh & Isobel Platt
Editor: Tim Leng
Assistant Editor: Samina Rahman
Production Manager:
Allison Gonsalves

Picture Credits: iStock

THINGS TO DO NOW THAT YOU'RE A GRANDPARENT

INTRODUCTION

It's finally happened! You are, at long last, a grandparent! Why do so many grandparents say if they had known it would be so great, they would have become a grandparent first? Because it's one of the most unique, enjoyable and rewarding roles you will ever play – most grandparents love the freedom of more choices and less responsibility when it comes to their relationships with grandchildren. The joys of sharing family history, hobbies, travels and just having fun with your grandchildren will fill your life with a renewed vitality and vigour.

Looking for creative new ways to connect with grandkids and support their parents? You're in the right place. Your instincts will kick in and you will probably be quite surprised at the things you'll do with those precious children – activities you never thought you'd be doing! Grandchildren will motivate you to try new things and to be the absolute best you can be.

Just like any role in life, there will be challenges as well as joys – from baby equipment and discipline to caregiving, family relationships, technology, and simply trying to keep energetic children and moody teens occupied. And you can bet that some things have changed since you raised your children. Not to worry! Including loads of great ideas, experiences and tips to help you build strong relationships with all your grandchildren, *Things to do Now That You're...a GRANDPARENT* will help you navigate this new, incredibly fulfilling world!

Tell your grandchildren you love them every chance you get. Your unconditional love is magic to a grandchild, and that's what they will remember about you the most.

Let your grandchildren be themselves. They are wonderful, unique people from the time they are born, and you will always love them for whom they are.

Show up – just being there for your grandchildren's school events, performances, games and matches will tell them how important they are to you.

LET YOUR GRANDCHILDREN KNOW YOU'RE NOT PERFECT, AND IT'S OK THAT THEY AREN'T EITHER.

Have a hugging contest to determine who gives the best hugs – you or your grandchild? No matter who wins, you'll both get lots of nice hugs in the process.

Practice active listening skills with your grandchildren: maintain eye contact, don't interrupt, ask questions, focus, and reflect or repeat back what was heard.

TELL YOUR GRANDCHILDREN HOW IMPORTANT THEY ARE TO YOU THROUGHOUT THEIR LIVES.

Building things together is a great way to bond with your grandchildren. A birdhouse is a great first project. Break down the work, so your grandchild gets to participate as much as you do - kids can only watch so much before they need to be actively involved.

SEND YOUR GRANDCHILDREN NOTES, CARDS AND LETTERS VIA 'SNAIL MAIL'.

Be your grandchild's 'safe place'. Be the warm, loving, nurturing person they can feel comfortable with when they are hurting, sad, lonely or tired.

Just hang out. That's right, do 'nothing' with your grandchildren. No plans, no schedule - just go with the flow and be together. Those times spent hanging out may be some of the sweetest moments you have together.

Share the lessons of your heart with your grandchildren. Tell them about a time you had your feelings hurt, what you learned and how you came out of it OK.

Keep a journal for each grandchild with anecdotes about things they say or do. As they get older, share the stories with them. They will love to hear about themselves, and will also see how important they are to you.

Teach your grandchildren to meditate! Keep it simple: for young ones, take just a few minutes and focus on breathing together. As they get older, introduce other meditative techniques.

Bedtime rituals are a time-honoured tradition. They help children chill out and settle down for sleep. Stick with whatever works best for them – a bath, a story, a massage or music. You may also want to add some special loving touches to their bedtime routine.

Share special little rituals with your grandchild. Create a special hug or handshake, close a conversation the same way each time, or try a unique sign-off on your emails to each other. Whatever you choose, it's just between you two.

It's sometimes hard to connect with older grandchildren, especially in those awkward teenage years. Even if they say something hurtful, don't let it get to you. Remind yourself that they will grow out of this phase.

COMMUNICATE WITH YOUR GRANDKIDS OFTEN AND TREAT THEM WITH RESPECT.

How do you want to be remembered by your family? Think about how your character may be perceived by your grandchildren and let them see your best side.

Ask your grandchildren to tell you stories. It shows you care about what goes on in their lives and helps them to explore their creative side.

Encourage self-expression. Create a safe environment where your grandchildren can express themselves as individuals.

Treat your grandchildren as equals when you talk with them. Always meet them at their level and relate to them respectfully.

Keep cool, but don't freeze – a great motto to have and teach to your grandchildren. You will undoubtedly hit some rough spots as a grandparent, but it's important to remain calm. If your grandchildren do something you don't agree with, don't freeze them out. Stay warm and loving towards them no matter what.

Your grandchildren all have different personalities, and some may be stronger or more outgoing than others. At family gatherings, make sure the quieter ones don't go unnoticed.

If you don't see your grandchildren very often, don't be hurt if they are not comfortable or cry when they first see you. Be kind and loving and they will soon warm to you.

Surprise!

Everyone loves surprises and your grandchildren are no exception. Surprise them with positive comments, phone calls, visits, presents and snuggles.

Always be generous in demonstrating your affections with hugs and snuggles if your grandchildren like them. Your grandchildren need lots of affection to grow up strong, confident and happy. And YOU are the perfect person to give it to them.

Comfort your grandchildren when they cry. It's good for them to know that they are not alone in the world and that love and healing are always out there.

Grandchild on the way? Hit the secondhand shops for some great deals on the basics that will make your home baby-friendly.

Keep track of your family's important events by starting an online family calendar that everyone can access from anywhere.

Get a good quality car seat for your car – your grandchildren's parents won't have to transfer their car seat back and forth when you babysit.

Your grandchildren are stars! Be sure you're ready to capture all the precious

moments spent together.

Take your grandchildren out to see the world. If you're into cycling tours, a rear child seat is the ideal vantage point for your grandchild to watch the world go by.

ARE YOU A RUNNER? GET A JOGGING BUGGY FOR YOUR YOUNGER GRANDCHILDREN – THEY'LL BE HAPPY TO GO ALONG FOR THE RIDE.

Get wired. If you don't have a personal computer – get one. If you have one but it's not up-to-date – upgrade! You'll want the latest and the greatest to organize, learn, communicate and savour every moment of being a grandparent.

Make your home kid-friendly! Create a play corner. It will make visits a lot easier for mum and dad when they don't have to bring entertainment from their own home.

Ask your grandchild's parents for advice about products and conveniences you'd like to get for your home. Things change rapidly when it comes to children and the equipment that comes along with them.

KEEP A SUPPLY OF CRAYONS, COLOURING BOOKS AND BLANK PAPER, SO YOUR GRANDCHILDREN CAN CREATE THEIR OWN WORKS OF ART.

UPDATE YOUR DRIVING SKILLS! IF YOU ARE DRIVING GRANDCHILDREN AROUND, YOU REALLY DO HAVE PRECIOUS CARGO ONBOARD.

Are you ready for meals with your new grandchild? Stock up on baby bottles, beakers, child-sized cutlery and dishes. Unbreakable is the key word when it comes to feeding time.

BEFORE THE LITTLE ONES COME TO VISIT, WALK SLOWLY THROUGH EACH ROOM IN YOUR HOME AND LOOK FOR SAFETY HAZARDS.

You probably got along fine raising your children without a mobile phone, but having one when you take your grandchildren on outings is a must.

A pint-sized chair, which is a perfect fit for your grandchild, will make them feel right at home. You can find rocking chairs just for kids, or even nicely stuffed armchairs just their size.

Pets are important members of many families. Take the time to carefully familiarize your grandchildren with your pets, and teach them both how to interact safely and lovingly with each other.

Summertime is a great season to be out in the garden. Buy some outdoor games, like croquet or lawn tennis, or a paddling pool and a beach ball to toss around. They have all winter to be inside.

GET SOME PAINTS AND DECORATE A FLOWERPOT WITH YOUR GRANDCHILDREN, THEN PLANT SOME SEEDS OR A SMALL HOUSEPLANT.

Race for it! If you want your grandchild to do something, turn it into a race to see who gets it done first.

Plant a garden with your grandchildren. Water and weed together. As your garden grows, so will your relationship.

What was your favourite game as a child? Your most treasured toys? There are many original vintage games and toys available now, or newly made imitations. Get your favourites and introduce them to your grandchildren. Some things are just classics, and you'll enjoy the memories they bring back of your own childhood.

Gather some wood, a hammer, nails and glue, and build a tree house for your grandchildren. Better yet, build it together. Make it your grandchildren's special place in your garden.

Go all out and create some spectacular ice-cream sundaes. Get creative about the toppings, including traditional hot fudge sauce as well as unusual things, like cereal, jam or brightly coloured sweets. Let your grandkids make their own sundae and watch them get creative with their toppings.

MAKE STORYTELLING A TRIP IN YOUR IMAGINATION – THE MORE OUTLANDISH THE BETTER!

Make up secret, silly nicknames for each other. Peanut, huggy bear, pickle nose, nano, top pop – whatever the two of you can agree upon. The sillier the better.

Plan a family talent show – or better yet – a 'no talent' show! See who can put on the worst act and offer a fun prize for the winner.

Teach your grandchildren about one of your hobbies. You may collect coins, watch movies, ski, cycle, fix cars, sew or garden. Whatever it is, bring it to their level and give them a glimpse of the things you really enjoy doing. You may end up with a hobby in common.

Be spontaneous! Sometimes the best memories are created out of unplanned moments of adventure and joy.

What game can you play without a board or props? Hide and seek! All homes have hiding places for young children, and don't forget to pretend you can't see them.

Everyone loves the movies! Co-produce a home video with your grandchild. The finished product will be something you can watch over and over again.

Learn a new skill with your grandchild. Starting out at the same level allows you to learn together, instead of one of you being the teacher.

Don't be afraid to cheer on your favourite sports team with your grandchildren. Get them a t-shirt or hat that matches yours and they'll be your biggest fans.

Have fun with your grandchild while also getting into shape. Skipping together will help your grandchild burn off excess energy and help you burn off calories.

Got water? Got balloons? Why not have water balloon fights with your grandchildren? They'll love getting soaked without getting into trouble, and even more, they'll enjoy getting you wet.

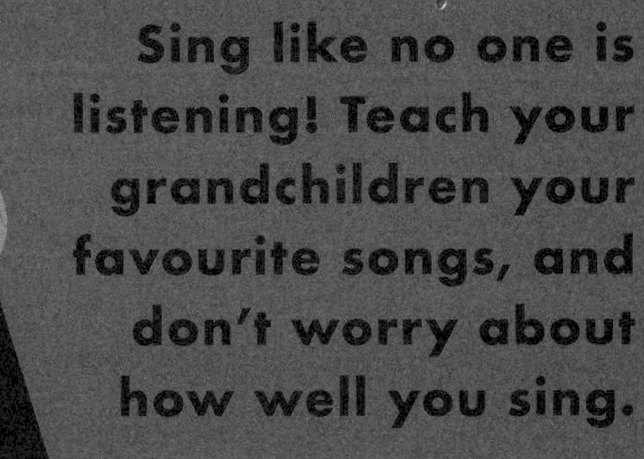

Sing like no one is listening! Teach your grandchildren your favourite songs, and don't worry about how well you sing.

HAVE A TICKLING CONTEST. WHO CAN GO THE LONGEST WITHOUT LAUGHING? REMEMBER, IT SHOULD BE FUN, SO KNOW WHEN ENOUGH IS ENOUGH.

Teach your grandchild how to make a bouquet of flowers. Pick them from your garden, or go to the florist together and pick out your favourites.

Soap it up! Collect small pieces of leftover soap, put them in a blender along with a little scented oil or some dried herbs, and add a little water. Blend well. Put the mixture in an ovenproof glass dish and heat gently. Pour the mixture into a mould and let it solidify. Voilà! You and your grandchild are soap-makers.

Create a lantern out of a gourd or pumpkin for some old-fashioned fun. Who needs to wait for Halloween to make a jack-o-lantern? Carve out flowers or other designs and insert a candle.

Make simple home-made finger paints with two cups of flour, two cups of cold water and food colouring. Get out the paper and let the kids have fun! Be prepared for brightly coloured little fingers, but it will wash off, eventually.

Bird-watch in your own garden! Give your grandchildren their very own set of binoculars and a children's bird book, and keep a notebook handy to record each time you see a different species of bird.

Practice insect 'catch and release' with your grandkids by helping them collect bugs, caterpillars, worms and other creepy crawlies in a glass jar. Take photos, look up the insects on the Internet and help them make their own bug book. When you've finished, release the critters back to nature.

TAKE YOUR GRANDCHILD WITH YOU TO VOLUNTEER AT THE LOCAL ANIMAL SHELTER. THEY'LL LEARN ABOUT GIVING BACK AND HAVE FUN WITH THE PUPS AT THE SAME TIME.

ONCE IN A WHILE, HAVE DESSERT AS A FIRST COURSE. YOUR GRANDCHILDREN WILL LOVE THE SURPRISE.

Have a silly supper with your grandchildren with a menu of whatever is in your cupboard, even if it absolutely does not go together or seem like a meal. Macaroni and cheese and pickles, leftover pizza and ice cream, hot dogs, pancakes and black olives. Be creative – the sillier the better.

Do you have a tradition of making certain favourite family recipes? Take time to teach your grandchildren how to make them. Make it an annual ritual, and as they grow older they'll take pride in knowing how to make the time-tested traditional recipes everyone loves.

Go for a picnic! Picnics are inexpensive and enough of an event to make a fuss over. Whether you picnic on the living room floor, your own garden or a beautiful park, it's a change of scenery and makes even everyday food taste special.

When was the last time you squeezed lemons to make your own lemonade? Try it with your grandchildren – it's a sticky, sweet delight that they'll enjoy because they helped make it.

Your youngest grandchildren can help you wash vegetables under cold water. Let them know what an important job they have, and then find something else for them to do while you cut the veggies.

Setting the table can be a fun activity – not just a chore. Allow your grandchildren to experiment with different tablecloths and napkins, dishes and table décor. Who cares if the knife and fork aren't in the right spots – they are creating a work of art.

Making cutout biscuits is a popular grandparent and grandchild activity. Try making the dough ahead of time, then have your grandchild help roll and cut the cookies. Make the icing together. It takes less time and still involves plenty of measuring and stirring, and your grandchild can get creative with colours.

Make bread with your grandchildren. Kneading dough by hand is a great way to burn off excess energy, and when the dough rises it's like a miracle - no matter what your age.

EVERY COOK NEEDS AN APRON! GET A PLAIN WHITE CHILD-SIZED CHEF APRON AND DECORATE IT YOURSELF WITH YOUR GRANDCHILD'S NAME.

Got 'cabin fever' during the winter? Bring some green into your home by planting a herb garden with your grandchildren.

Making jams and jellies is becoming a lost art. Why not make some with your grandchildren?

Have a 'sleep-tight-nighty-night' holiday pyjama tradition. Give your grandchildren special festive pyjamas for each holiday. They'll anticipate them each holiday season, and they won't want that tradition to end even after they are out of footy pyjamas.

Create your grandchild's own calendar, including events like their first day of big school, the date they scored their first football goal or even their first date. Celebrate the big and the little triumphs in their lives.

Celebrate holidays, but on the wrong dates. Have a Christmas celebration in July, or Halloween in April. Your grandkids will love the silliness of it.

While traditions are important, they sometimes become outdated. Don't hang on to those that aren't working. Cherish the memories of them, and create new traditions that fit in with the different interests and ages of your grandchildren.

Create a special ornament for the holidays with a photo of you and your grandchild – it will trigger many happy memories in your grandchild's future.

As your family grows, it may be necessary to change traditions and holiday celebrations. Deal with it. Adapt and go with the flow. Just do your best to ensure your grandchildren remember the holidays as a time of family togetherness and fun.

Help your grandchildren learn that holidays aren't just about getting expensive gifts. If you have some craft supplies, make home-made gifts for them.

Children love parties – big and small. Holidays are a great excuse for a party. Pull out the noisemakers, decorations, candles and cake, and you've got a celebration.

GO GREEN – TEACH YOUR GRANDCHILDREN ABOUT RECYCLING.

Volunteer with your grandchildren and help them learn the ethic of volunteering and service through action.

Teach your grandchildren about conservation by starting a compost pile in your yard. When they visit, have them collect eggshells, coffee grounds, leaves and other goodies for the pile. Be sure to have them help spread the compost on your garden in the spring, so they can see the results.

Children are little explorers. Their natural curiosity will spur them to venture where no one has gone before...or at least no child. While you want to keep them safe, try not to dampen their enthusiastic curiosity – in fact, nurture it! It will serve them well in life.

Start a book club with your grandchildren. You might be surprised at how much you enjoy reading the books they like, and you'll have some really good conversations.

Listen to your grandchildren read – be their best audience. Not only will you enjoy it, your patience and attention will help them learn.

Parlez-vous another language? Teach your grandchildren words and phrases in your second tongue from an early age. The younger they learn, the faster they learn.

Stock up on children's activity books that include stories to read and games to play, which make learning fun. Keep them on hand at your house and when on the go.

Did you learn the ABC's or other language skills by singing a well-known song? And you still remember it, don't you? If you want your grandkids to remember something, become a composer and set it to music.

Visit a museum that has a 'hands-on' exhibit to make history come to life. Being able to dig like an archaeologist, wear clothes from the 17th century, play with toys from long ago, or plant seeds in the manner planters did thousands of years ago is a lot more engaging than looking at things through a glass window. An interactive activity is an exciting learning experience for your grandchildren.

Do you sew? Teach your grandchildren to sew. They'll learn spatial awareness skills when they place patterns on the fabric, and their dexterity and creativity will get a boost too.

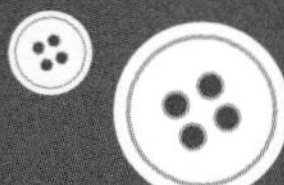

Teach your grandchildren to read maps. Let them guide you to the shops, the campsite, the holiday destination or around your own garden.

Play chess with your grandchildren. It helps them develop thinking and reasoning skills while playing a cool classic game.

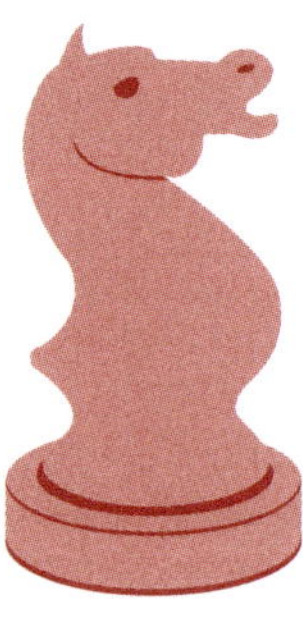

Are your grandchildren interested in nature? There are many activities you can do with them to draw out their naturalistic talents - hiking, gardening, visiting animal farms and researching dinosaurs are just a few.

Learn some basic sign language and teach your grandchildren how to sign with you, so you can have a special form of communication between the two of you.

Fill a big basket with musical instruments that your grandchildren can use at any time. Not collector's items, just percussion instruments, wooden flutes and other inexpensive instruments. They'll learn all kinds of good skills, and will also have fun filling the minutes with music.

HAVE A FAMILY SPELLING CONTEST. ONCE YOUR YOUNGER GRANDCHILDREN START LEARNING TO READ AND WRITE THEY CAN PARTICIPATE ALSO.

The library is a great place to spend a rainy afternoon with your grandchildren. Most libraries have a children's story hour for younger kids, and older kids will also be able to find books they like.

Follow the weather with your grandchild. Learn about cumulus clouds and how rain is made. Study snowflakes and thunderstorms. Weather makes science tangible.

Make a boat with your grandchildren. Try it out in the bathtub first to make sure it floats, then take it to a stream, river or lake near you.

Go fly a kite or paper aeroplane with your grandchild! They will learn about air patterns, gravity and wind – and have loads of fun in the process.

Play 'Twenty Questions' with your grandchildren whenever you have some time to kill. It will help them learn at least twenty things about whatever object or person you choose.

FUN FACTS, QUIZZES AND WORD GAMES WILL HELP YOUR GRANDCHILD LEARN EXCELLENT THINKING, LOGIC AND ANALYTICAL SKILLS.

Teach your grandchildren about world geography by hanging a large world map in your home. Every time they visit, let them pick a place in the world that they would like to discover.

Visit your childhood home with your grandchildren. Show them the places you used to go and tell them real stories that took place there to spur their imaginations.

Take your grandchildren to the beach and help them build the biggest, most amazing sandcastle they've ever seen.

Visit a farm with your grandchildren and 'pick your own'. Apples, berries, peaches and pumpkins are all tastier when you've gathered or picked them yourself.

You don't have to go away to have fun. Hold a sleepover party at your house. Invite your grandchildren over and get out the blankets and sleeping bags. Watch movies, eat popcorn, play games and stay up late with them.

Take a train ride with your grandchildren – even a short ride is fun for younger kids. Take the time to watch the trains, examine how they work, talk to a conductor, get a treat at the train station and take some photos.

IS THERE A HARBOUR NEAR YOU? A DOCK OR MOORING IS WORTH A VISIT TO LOOK AT THE BOATS, WATCH THE FISHERMEN AND TALK ABOUT LIFE ON THE WATER.

Visit the local fire station. Firefighters are usually quite willing to show the children the fire engines, where they eat and sleep and what to do if they are ever in a fire.

When was the last time you went to a rock concert? Ask your grandchild who their favourite band is and get tickets for the two of you. Open your mind and find something you like about your grandchild's music. Then switch it – take your grandchild to a concert of one of your favourites.

Amusement parks are a favourite family holiday destination. Plan your trip carefully so your energy levels coordinate with your grandchildren's and everyone has fun.

Collect a pebble or rock from each special outing you go on with your grandchildren. Keep them in a special jar or dish. When they visit, you can go through the rocks and remember all the great places you've been together.

A science museum is a great place to visit on a rainy afternoon. Your grandchildren will be fascinated by the great hands-on experiments the museum has to offer.

Gather up the grandchildren and go to a live sporting event. For little ones, it won't matter if it's the local school football game or a major cup event. The sights, sounds, scents and action will all seem marvellous to them.

Hiking is a great way to introduce and teach your grandchildren about nature. It's also a fun way to get your grandchildren to exercise.

ASK YOUR GRANDCHILDREN FOR THEIR INPUT AS YOU GET READY TO GO ON AN ADVENTURE WITH THEM. IF THEY HELP YOU PLAN THE TRIP, THEY'LL GET MORE EXCITED AS THEY ANTICIPATE THE HOLIDAY.

Trips and travel don't have to break your budget. Most children will not remember the money you spend; they'll remember the good times you had together.

Get out the tents and sleeping bags and go camping or caravanning. Even if you camp in your own garden.

It's nice for grandchildren to get one-on-one time with grandma and grandpa. Plan a unique trip for each grandchild. Each child will feel special getting your undivided attention, and it will help you get to know them better.

TAKE YOUR GRANDCHILD TO SEE A LIVE PLAY OR MUSICAL. TURN IT INTO A SPECIAL AFTERNOON TREAT AND GO TO LUNCH OR TEA.

FESTIVALS AND FAIRS ARE FUN TO VISIT WITH GRANDCHILDREN BECAUSE YOU NEVER KNOW WHAT YOU WILL FIND THERE.

Always carry snacks and supplies with you when you travel with your grandchildren. Even a short day trip will require some backup food.

Tread gently when you talk with your children about your grandchildren. Always remember that they are the parents and you'll have a better relationship with them and your grandchildren if you respect their choices.

Your family is a melting pot of viewpoints, experiences, personalities and lifestyles, and you as a grandparent are the connector that brings your amazing family together on common ground.

Tell your grandchildren about your parents, so they will know how important they were to you and have a sense of the generations that came before them.

Tell your grandchildren stories about their parents. Kids love this, especially the funny things their parents did or said when they were younger.

Listen to your children when they need to talk about parenting and your grandchildren. Your role is not to judge, it is to love and support.

WHEN IT COMES TO DISAGREEMENTS BETWEEN GRANDPARENTS AND PARENTS, FOCUS ON WHAT IS IN THE BEST INTEREST OF THE GRANDCHILD.

Want some family interaction? Bring out the cards and board games. They don't have to be complicated games to get the competition and laughter going, and you'll find that different generations will relate to each other in the process.

Pets are part of the family, too. If you have cats, dogs, birds or other pets, get your grandkids to feed and care for them. They'll learn the importance of being responsible pet-owners.

Tell your grandchildren funny stories about yourself when you were growing up, especially the embarrassing ones.

Ever thought about writing your memoir? Do it! Get down on paper the key experiences in your life, what you've learned, the work you've done and the people you've known. There are books and websites devoted to memoir writing that are a great source to guide you.

Gather your family together on a regular basis. Even if some family members can't be there, the ritual of gathering as a family will be remembered fondly by your grandchildren in years to come, and hopefully they'll carry on the tradition themselves.

Make a phone call just to your grandchild. They'll feel special that you called just to talk to them. If they don't feel like talking, don't take it personally – some kids are just not phone people.

Give your grandchildren self-addressed stamped envelopes and note paper. Ask them to send you a note or drawing once a month, and enlist their parents to help out.

Make sure your grandchildren are aware of their cultural and ethnic backgrounds. Tell them stories, visit the places that are significant to your culture, read books and play games that reinforce their connection to their ancestors. Make it fun and they will be more eager to learn.

If you are a step-grandparent, make it clear that you are not trying to replace your grandchildren's biological grandmother or grandfather. You can have a very special role in their lives, but may need to take a back seat now and then, and that's OK.

Caring for grandchildren can be a joyful as well as a stressful experience. Take a break and be kind to yourself if you need to. Looking after kids can be draining and you need to conserve your energy.

There are many great online resources for grandparents who care for grandchildren, whether you are babysitting, providing regular childcare or raising them full-time. Look out for online support groups, discussion boards, and chat rooms, as well as articles, advice columns, financial planning tools and more.

It can sometimes be hard to keep up with the demands of your grandchildren. Let them know that sometimes you need help too. It's OK to let them know that you are also vulnerable now and then.

It takes a whole family to raise a child. If you're playing a more prominent role in your grandkid's lives, don't hesitate to call upon extended family - aunts, uncles and cousins - for support.

THE MORE TIME YOU SPEND WITH YOUR GRANDCHILDREN, THE MORE YOU WILL PLAY A ROLE IN THEIR LIVES.

Does your grandchild have a savings account? If not, check with their parents to be sure they're OK with it, and open one. Seed the account with an initial gift, and add some to it on a regular basis, or on birthdays or holidays. When your grandchild grows up, it will be a wonderful gift to have a nest egg that will help them with education, their first car or living expenses.

Teach your grandchildren how to save by helping them create both short-term goals (saving for a toy or ice cream) and long-term goals (saving for a bike, an expensive video game, computer or university).

Give the gift of music. Talk it over with your grandchildren's parents, and offer to pay for piano, violin, drum or voice coaching lessons. It's an extra that many parents can't afford, and it will enrich your grandchildren's lives.

Saving for the grandkids is no different to saving for a car or house renovation. The earlier you start to put money aside, the more financially stable you'll be.

When your grandchild goes to university, you may want to treat them somehow to help them on their path to earning a degree.

Keep a penny jar. Every time you think of your grandchild, put a penny in the jar. Each night empty your pockets into the jar. When the jar is full, take it to the bank and make a deposit in a savings account for your grandchild. You'll be surprised how quickly coins add up.

CASH SLIPPED INTO A BIRTHDAY CARD OR POCKET IS ALWAYS A WELCOME GIFT.

ALLOW YOUR GRANDCHILDREN TO MAKE MISTAKES WITH MONEY. MISTAKES ARE REALLY JUST LEARNING EXPERIENCES IN DISGUISE.

PLANT A TREE IN YOUR GRANDCHILD'S NAME. THE TWO OF YOU CAN WATCH 'THEIR' TREE GROW OVER THE YEARS.

The most important gift you will ever give your grandchildren doesn't come in a box or package. It can't be wrapped in pretty paper. Your greatest gift is your time, attention and love – that's what they really need.

Put yourself on a holiday shopping budget when buying gifts for grandchildren. It's easy to go overboard and either overload them with more gifts than they can appreciate, or overload your bank account.

It is OK to say 'no' to grandchildren. Refusing to buy gifts you can't afford, that aren't age-appropriate or they are not allowed to have is acceptable. They'll get over it.

Gifts are about receiving as well as giving. Be a graceful recipient of whatever your children and grandchildren choose to give you.

Have a holiday gift-making party with your grandchildren. Everyone loves hand-made gifts, and their parents will be grateful for a break to go and do their own holiday shopping.

Consider giving your grandchildren the gift of experiences, rather than things. They'll eventually forget the things, but they'll remember the experiences and the skills they acquired for a lifetime.

MAKE SURE YOUR GRANDCHILDREN KNOW THAT YOU DON'T MEASURE LOVE BY THE NUMBER AND COST OF GIFTS RECEIVED.

Hold yourself back when it comes to presents for very young children. They really aren't that interested in all the presents they get – you'll often find they're more interested in playing with the wrapping paper.

When your grandchildren are young, it may be hard for siblings to watch the birthday child open all those wonderful presents. It's a nice idea to bring a small item for the non-birthday sibling to open, if parents are OK with it.

If your grandchildren's parents agree, offer to help the little ones go through their toys, games, dolls and stuffed animals. Help them donate the items that they don't play with anymore to children who don't have toys.

Help your grandchildren write thank-you notes to friends and family after their birthday or a holiday. They'll learn good manners and appreciate the presents they receive.

When buying gifts for grandchildren, keep the parents in mind. They may never forgive you if you buy your grandchild a drum set that will percussively fill their lives with constant loud drumming.

Consider giving your grandchildren the meaningful gift of a donation to a charitable cause. You can give an animal in their name that will help sustain a family in need in another country.

Save money each month for birthday and Christmas presents. Get a gift list in plenty of time, so you have money available for those highly desired gifts your grandchildren want so much.

TEACH YOUR GRANDCHILDREN THE VALUE OF MONEY. SET REALISTIC LIMITS.

UNCONDITIONAL
LOVE IS PRICELESS!
NO MATTER WHAT YOUR
GRANDCHILDREN DO,
MAKE SURE THEY
KNOW YOU
LOVE THEM.